# A  brides guide to her photographer

Paul e langford

# DEDICATION

I decided to write this guide for all you brides to be after being a wedding photographer for some time,I myself admittedly made mistakes at my first wedding my two main cameras broke down and had to rely on a backup camera that wasn't suitable for taking high quality shots due to not having a good quality lens.on another wedding I relied on another person's equipment and was a sure he had had it serviced and cleaned only to find the lens were fury around the edges,I was lucky as I had enough space around the photo to edit or I

would have certainly been up
popular with the bride.
I went on to do a lot more
weddings with a successful
outcome learning as I went ,this
explains why ime confident this
guide for you  bride to be.

CONTENT

Bride and groom

ACKNOWLEDGMENTS
ADAM LANGFORD FOR
INSPIRATION IN WRITING THIS
MANUAL

# BRIDE AND GROOM

The time have come for you both to think about planning your future wedding together,flowers,cake,disco,band ,honeymoon,rings,cars,and more,and of course
your wedding photographer so you will be able to remember

your wedding in years to come .
When you visit and buy your wedding dress you will probably notice wedding photos on the walls you've probably guessed it by now they will offer you a photographers number mainly because they or on commission.

If you approach this photographer yourself you will be able to save the discount you would be paying to the wedding dress supplier.

Everybody is out to make money at after all a wedding

means  over priced goods from flowers to tiaras, don't tell the florist the flowers are for a wedding and they will be much lower in price and this also goes for the reception , phone up first and price it then phone up in another name and see if there is a difference I'll  be surprised if they isn't , now back to your photographer you probably know that the groom mostly selects the photographer ask yourself why I suppose  your husband to be is a photographer I think probably not is your husband   to   be   friend   a photographer probably not but I do expect his friend has a digital camera and has a collection of stunning photos this may make him a good photographer but not your wedding photographer,it is a little like when having a barbecue you cook all year round then your husband comes out cooks a burger and takes all the glory ,but can he cook probably not so why leave him in charge of the photographer for the most important day of your life, he doesn't and have no real intension of ruining the wedding but I expect he's thinking of all the money he could save ,but is it worth it all that anxiety it will bring between you both.

A knock on the door and your photographer have arrived open the door and see how he greets you after all this is how he will be greeting the guests invite him in and offer coffee tea or something a little stronger like beer or a whiskey, let's face it if he goes for the alcohol there's now way your photographer is going to be still standing by mid afternoon with all the offers he will receive in the reception I guess you can ask him to leave now, tell him why maybe he will alter his ways leading to being a better photographer.

well if he's passed this test make him or her a coffee and proceed to they attire, tee shirts jeans ,trainers , etc is a big no we want shirts suits polished shoes boots etc clean shaved with a nice aftershave or perfume after all if he she smells how close will your guests want to be ,if you happy start question him her about their photographic kit have they brought it with them I certainly would want to see the camera flashguns, after ask him what type of cameras he uses and what size megapixel ask if he uses a full frame camera (best d.s.l.r.),does he have back up cameras flashgun batteries does he have a assistant to take candid shots of all guests most photographers today will have one or more assistant depending on the quantity of guests, due to having digital camera's they could take around two hundred to a one thousand photos per wedding ,out of all of these only fifty of the best shots will be used also state what type of photography you will want modern or traditional a good photographer will be able to provide you with a portfolio of both and give you a CD with all of them on, this will save you a lot of money as later on you will want to have enlargements done for you and your family if you haven't a CD with all your pictures on then you will have to pay the over inflated prices your photographer charges so having this CD is a must in the price .

Did he arrive with a portfolio if he has not ask him why as it's the first thing you would pick up when going to a potential client if he has, take a look does he have traditional and modern albums ask for proof they his photos as it's very easy to download from Google image these days print out your albums and there you are a photographer, but after reading this guide you will hopefully not be fooled into hiring a bogus photographer , one thing a big fat deposit ,never give a deposit unless very low after all he may not make it on the day and neither may you, always have your photos before handing over large sums of money ,always ask if your photos will be printed or developed, printing can be far better quality thanks to the digital age  but only if the printer uses light fast pigment ink and printed with ten colour printers on archival paper. this will grantee the prints will  last for as long g as two hundred years by now you should have the confidence to pick your photographer and be assured you will have the pictures you wished far so I wish you all the best for your future together as husband and wife

# My other books

I started to write after suffering from gout and spent a number of months laid up in bed, I realised I would not be going back to manual work so started writing about thing I have done in my life, I have a series children's books being released soon called Adventures of Toby the caravan.

Toby is a run down caravan who lives all all alone on a chicken farm in a  South Wales valley when the farm becomes a home for a caravan club Toby becomes a hero on many adventures with all his new friends who also have  adventures on and of the farm, the first book introduces the farm farmer and caravans Diesel is from France and have a powerful engine with a stink a that comes from  garlic that he grows on the roof disco has speakers all around him and is always playing music ,stealth is the night such rite caravan and can not be seen at due to his blacked out windows and doors, built with cameras on  all sides and the latest surveillance protects the yard and everyone in it these are only a fuel of many in a series of stories being released soon be sure not to let your little ones miss out hard copy available to.

My other book soon to be released is adventures of a south Wales valley boy a true story of how I grew up and the things I got up to some good some not so good ,i have decided to write this as I have children of my own

and living on the Dorset
coast and with today's laws
and society it would be
impossible for a boy to have
the adventure and freedom
that I had from my first
airgun at ten and motorbike
at eleven only to be ridden
around the housing estate
and up to the mountains
,and how I made my own
Molotov cocktails ,but open
army bullets , you will have

to read the book as I can assure you will wonder how on earth ime here to tell the story.

If for any reason you would like to contact me you may do so by using the email below ,,,,,,,,,,,,,,

Paullangford.pl@gmail.com

please feel free to leave your

comments for future reference

Paullangford.pl@gmail.com